ON THE MAKING OF A

GOOD CONTRACT

K.V. NARAYANMURTI, BA, BL, FICA

About the Author

Shri Narayan Murti is a highly accomplished expert in the field of legal issues and contracts. With a wealth of experience and expertise, he has made significant contributions to the legal profession, corporate world, and academia throughout his distinguished career.

Shri Narayan Murti began his journey in law after enrolling in the Madras Bar as an Advocate in the High Court in 1962. His early years were marked by his exceptional skills in labor union negotiations, arbitration, and conciliation. His profound understanding of industrial relations and his ability to navigate complex issues in this domain earned him a reputation as a seasoned administrator and negotiator.

During his professional journey, Shri Narayan Murti had the privilege of working as Secretary & Chief Accountant, working closely with the esteemed founders of Larsen and Toubro (L&T), Mr. Henning Holck-Larsen and Mr. Soren Kristian Toubro.

His close association with both Danish entrepreneurs provided him with valuable insights into international business practices and expanded his network of connections. This experience instilled in him a deep understanding of corporate dynamics and laid the foundation for his successful experience in corporate law.

Shri Narayan Murti held a prominent Board-level position and served as the Managing Director of Indian Transformers Limited, a wholly-owned subsidiary of GEC (General Electric Company). His tenure at GEC showcased his exceptional leadership abilities and strategic vision in transforming businesses.

Following his retirement, Shri Narayan Murti chose to share his vast knowledge and experience in corporate law by establishing a legal practice specializing in corporate laws. Simultaneously, he served as a professor at Vidya Bhavan, where he taught courses on Indian culture and industrial relations.

His teaching engagements allowed him to shape the minds of aspiring legal professionals, imparting not only legal knowledge but also the importance of cultural understanding within the realm of industrial relations.

Shri Narayan Murti's passion for literature and writing led him to contribute as a columnist for The Indian Express, where he critically reviewed numerous books. This endeavor showcased his intellectual acumen and analytical prowess, further establishing him as a respected authority in the legal and literary circles.

Beyond his legal and academic pursuits, Shri Narayan Murti has been a successful investor, demonstrating his astute business acumen in turning around struggling companies and ventures.

His ability to identify key opportunities and provide expert guidance has made him a sought-after advisor for both industrialists and government bureaucrats heading major organizations.

He has actively resolved complex issues related to corporate laws and industrial relations, consistently showcasing his expertise as a problem solver.

Throughout his illustrious career, Shri Narayan Murti has earned the admiration of his peers, professors, and students alike. His exceptional performance in law school not only secured him a gold medal and high rank but also established enduring relationships with prominent jurists who later became eminent Judges in State High Courts and the Supreme Court. His wide network of admirers extends across the world, a testament to his global impact and influence.

Contents

- ➢ Discharge of Contracts

- ➢ Act of God, `Force Majeure`

- ➢ Frustration

- ➢ Time as essence of the Contract

- ➢ Some thumb rules in Contract Management

Breach of Contract & Remedies

Arbitration

Enforcement of Arbitral Awards

On Engagement of Contract Labour

Preface

The law of contract is an essential pillar of any legal system, governing the obligations that individuals willingly undertake. It presupposes a society where people possess the freedom to choose the obligations they wish to assume, thus reflecting the principles of personal autonomy and voluntary exchange. However, as modern societies continue to evolve economically and socially, the importance of a comprehensive law of contract becomes increasingly evident.

The division of labor, a fundamental characteristic of our modern societies, generates a growing need for the transfer of property and the provision of services between individuals. These transactions form the bedrock of our economic interactions, and the legal framework that facilitates these transfers and services is, in essence, the law of contract.

It serves as the guiding force behind the methods by which goods and services are exchanged, typically in return for monetary compensation.

Nevertheless, the mere presence of good intentions is insufficient to create a solid and enforceable contract. Proper expressions and documentation are crucial elements in ensuring that contractual agreements are clear, unambiguous, and legally sound. Familiarizing oneself with the legal aspects of basic contract law becomes imperative in this pursuit.

This book aims to provide a comprehensive understanding of the intricacies involved in crafting a good contract. By delving into the nuances of contract law, readers will gain valuable insights into the essential elements, principles, and best practices necessary to create robust and effective agreements.

From the formation and interpretation of contracts to the rights and obligations of the parties involved, this book serves as a practical guide for navigating the complexities of contract law.

Whether you are a business professional, an aspiring entrepreneur, a legal practitioner, or simply an individual seeking to enhance your understanding of contractual relationships, this book offers a valuable resource. By equipping yourself with the knowledge presented within these pages, you will be better prepared to engage in contractual arrangements with confidence and safeguard your interests.

It is my hope that this book will serve as a reliable companion, offering clarity and guidance, as you embark on your journey towards The.

K.V. Narayanmurti,

Advocate & Corporate Laws Advisor

The making of a good contract

Introduction:

Broadly speaking, the law of Contract is that part of the law which deals with obligations which are self-imposed. It pre-supposes a society and a legal system in which people have the right to choose what obligations they wish to assume.

With the economic and social development of modern societies, the need for a law of contract becomes far more pressing for at least two reasons. In the first place, the division of labour, which is such a fundamental feature of modern societies, creates an increasing demand for the transfer of property from some members of the community to others and for the performance of services by some members of the community for others. The legal machinery by which these transfers of property and performance of services is carried out is, broadly speaking, the law of contract.

Contract law is thus, in large part the law of exchange, the law which regulates the methods by which individuals exchange goods and services usually in return for money.

Good intentions do not always make a good contract. Proper expressions and documentation, help. For this purpose, it is necessary to familiarize oneself with the legal aspects of basic contract law.

What is a contract?

The most accepted description of a contract is "a promise or a set of promises which the law will enforce". The promise may be to act in a certain way as, for example, by rendering services or delivering goods or it may be a promise that something is so, as for example where a seller guarantees that goods are fit for a certain purpose. The law of contract determines which promises the law will enforce and how it will enforce them.

Promises, generally, may be enforceable though they are purely oral, in writing, by conduct or by a combination of two or three of these methods. A contract for the sale of goods of any value - say, diamonds worth Rs. 10 lacs - is enforceable though there is no writing. An important exception is a contract disposing of an interest in land.

Virtually all offers to contract can be reduced to the form: "I promise this if you will do, or promise to do, that". A contract is made when the promise does the act or makes the promise requested. The consideration is doing the act or making the promise, as the case may be. If the promisor asks for a promise, which is given, we describe the resulting contract as a "bilateral contract". I promise to pay you Rs. 1000/- a week from the beginning of next month if you will promise to work for me for a year. When you promise, the contract is made.

We describe it as "bilateral" because both parties have binding promise. The consideration for each promise is the making of the other promise.

Contracts, then, are bargains, and a natural way of concluding a bargain is by offer and acceptance. One party must first state the terms on which he is willing to be bound before the other can express his concurrence. The law looks for an offer and acceptance, not for some technical reasons, but because this is the natural, and often the only possible, way in which a bargain can be made. The essential thing is, however, the bargain and, if this can be discerned from the conduct of the parties, there is a contract even though it may be impossible to say who is the offeror and who the acceptor. As a general principle, an offer must be reasonably definite and require nothing to complete except acceptance. An offer also needs to be distinguished from a mere invitation to do business.

Duration of an offer:

An offeree's power of acceptance may be terminated by –

(a) Rejection or counteroffer by the offeree, or

(b)Lapse of time, or

(c)Revocation by the offeror, or

(d) Death or incapacity of the offeror or offeree, or

(e) The non-occurrence of any condition of acceptance

under the terms of the offer.

Acceptance

Acceptance must be absolute and unconditional and must

indicate a willingness to contract on the exact terms put

by the offeror. A purported acceptance which seeks to

add to, or vary some terms of the offer is, in law, no

acceptance at all although such a purported acceptance

can and will be treated as a counteroffer, itself capable of

acceptance. Moreover, a counteroffer amounts to a

rejection of the original offer, which then ceases to be

capable of acceptance.

These rules are somewhat rigid and may well be too rigid. It often happens that a person intends to accept an offer and writes a letter stating that he does accept it, but then adds some further remarks or some question (e.g., 'I presume payment by cheque will be acceptable) which may be relatively unimportant or trivial. But these further remarks or questions may be held to qualify the purported acceptance to such a degree that they prevent it having the legal character of an acceptance. The offeror may then be free to withdraw at the last minute.

If, however, he simply fails to reply to the additional remarks raised by the offeree, but proceeds with the performance of the contract, it may be possible to hold that the counter-offer has in turn been accepted by conduct. It follows, therefore, that a conditional acceptance may fail to count as a real acceptance at all.

Letters of intent:

It is these days not uncommon to find companies issuing 'letters of intent' recording their intention to enter into a formal agreement and requesting the addressee to take necessary preliminary steps towards the performance of that agreement. Such a letter of intent (when accepted or perhaps when relied upon) can itself be sufficient to create contractual liability, if there are no obvious and fundamental disagreements on the terms still to be negotiated.

Sanctity of a written contract:

Where the parties have reduced their contract to writing it is not permissible, as a general rule, to adduce oral evidence to add to, vary or contradict the written instrument. Similarly, neither party can rely on evidence extrinsic to the contractual document of terms alleged to have been agreed but not contained in the document.

But, if the written document was not intended to set out all the terms agreed between the parties, extrinsic evidence of the other terms is admissible.

Consideration:

Consideration means a reason for the enforcement of the law, may consist either in some rights, interest, profit, or benefit accruing to the one party, or some forbearance, detriment, loss, or responsibility, given, suffered, or undertaken by the other.

Therefore, an act or forbearance of the one party, or the promise thereof, is the price for which the promise of the other is bought, and the promise thus given for value, is enforceable. If the promisor gets what he asks for in return for his promise, he has received sufficient consideration and is bound.

It is immaterial that his promise is far more valuable than the price he has asked for it.

The courts are generally concerned only with the question whether the promisor has made a bargain, not with whether he has made a good bargain. They will not inquire into the adequacy of the consideration he has asked for and received, except when one party is able to take unfair advantage of another.

Effect of mistake in the making of offer or acceptance:

A contracting party who had made a mistake simply had himself to blame. Unless, of course, the mistake was induced by something said or done by the other party, in which case there might be remedies for fraud or misrepresentation or, perhaps, breach of a contractual term.

Statements made during negotiations for a contract and their effect:

It is common for one party to make statement during the course of negotiations for a contract with the object and, perhaps, the effect of inducing the other party to contract.

Sometimes, such statements may be held to amount to promises and to become part of the contract so that, if they are unfulfilled, an action for breach of contract will lie.

On other occasions, the statement will be held not to form part of the contract. For example, where a contract of sale has been reduced to writing, assurances which were given by the seller as to his goods, will probably be held not to form part of the contract, if they are not referred to in the document itself. The rule excluding oral evidence (where there is a written document) would apply to exclude evidence which would add to, vary or contradict the written document.

Implied terms:

The courts will generally enforce consequences logically implied in the language of the contracts. In fact, judges are accustomed to read into documents and transactions many terms that are not logically implied in them.

They may be broadly classified as

(i)   terms that the parties probably had in mind but

        did not trouble to express;

(ii)   terms that the parties, whether or not they

        actually had them in mind, would probably

        have expressed if the question had been brought

        to their attention and

(iii)   terms that the parties, whether or not they had

        them in mind or would have expressed them if

        they had foreseen the difficulty, are implied by

        the court because of the court's view of fairness

        or policy or in consequence of basic rules of

        law.

Of these three, the first is an effort to arrive at

actual intention, the second is an effort to arrive

at hypothetical or conditional intention - the

intention that the parties would have had, if

they had foreseen the difficulty and, the third is

not concerned with the intention of the parties,

except to the extent that the term implied by the

court may be excluded by an expression of positive intention to the contrary.

Consideration:

Only those promises which are supported by a legal consideration are legally binding; other promises are not binding even if the promisor intends to bind himself by his promise. Law distinguishes between gratuitous and non-gratuitous promises. The doctrine of 'Consideration' rests on two legs, the first is the idea that a promise is legally binding if it is given in return for some benefit which is rendered, or to be rendered, to the promisor. The second is the notion that a promise becomes binding if the promise incurs a detriment by relying upon it, that is, if he changes his position in reliance on the promise in such a way that he would be worse off if the promise is broken than he would have been if the promise had never been made at all.

NATURE AND EFFECT OF CONTRACTUAL TERMS

Condition and Warranty:

"Condition' is a promise in a contract of so important a nature that a failure to perform it entitles the other party to terminate the contract as well as to sue for damages. In contrast is "Warranty' which also is a promise, but one of a subsidiary nature, the breach of which entitles the injured party to damages only and, not to terminate the contract.

Jurisdiction:

An agreement purporting to oust the jurisdiction of the courts is illegal and void on grounds of public policy.

Capacity to Contract:

A corporation has necessarily to contract through an agent and, to avoid disputes as to the agent's authority, it is laid down that a contract by the corporation must be under seal, although it is not necessary that every one of its contracts should be under seal.

Similarly in case of partnership or Sole proprietorships, the contracts are to be executed by persons who have the specific authority to do so.

Discharge of Contracts:

The obvious mode of discharge is by performance, precise and exact. Or when one party is ready and willing and offers to perform the promise according to the agreed terms, but the other side refuses to accept the performance, the contract is discharged by tender, and the party who offered performance is excused from performance.

It may also happen that, owing to change of circumstances, both the contracting parties or (when one has performed his obligation) the party entitled to demand performance may be willing to waive it. The contract is then discharged by consent.

It may also be that, at the time when the parties entered into the contract, they knew or must have known that the contract was to be performed, only if a certain set of circumstances exists, and if circumstances are so altered that, what they bargained for could not be had, then, there ensues what in law is called "impossibility of performance". The basic idea of impossibility of performance as a mode of discharge, is really the implied understanding that the common object of the contract can no longer be achieved because, in the light of the circumstances, a situation fundamentally different from that contemplated when the parties entered into the contract has unexpectedly emerged. In such a case the party is excused from performance.

Finally, if a contract is not performed, or if the party entitled does not waive performance, or if there is no valid excuse for non-performance, then the other party becomes liable for breach of contract and the party entitled can sue for damages or claim specific performance, injunction etc.

Act of God, 'Force Majeure':

Generally defined as "an extra-ordinary occurrence or circumstance which could not have been guarded against, or more accurately, an accident due to natural causes, directly and exclusively, without human intervention and which could not have been avoided by any amount of foresight and care." In such cases also, a contract is discharged.

Frustration:

Performance is also excused where a fundamental assumption underlying the contract has become impossible in the sense that the substantial object which the parties had in view is no longer attainable.

The intention of the parties is frustrated owing to a supervening event since the contract was made.

The basis of the doctrine of frustration is that the parties have impliedly agreed that the contract when performed would be different from the contract as agreed to be performed, then the contract need not be performed.

Time as essence of the contract:

In Indian law, the question whether time is of the essence of the contract would essentially be a question of the intention of the parties to be gathered from the terms of the contract. Even where the parties have expressly if time is of the essence of the contract, such a stipulation will have to be read along with the other provisions of the contract. If the contract were to provide for, say, extension of time in certain contingencies or for payment of liquidated damages or penalty for every day or week the work remains unfinished, such clauses would be considered as rendering ineffective the express provision relating to time being of the essence of a contract.

The party accepting performance after the due date must give notice, while accepting, that he intends to claim compensation, otherwise he is deemed to have waived such right.

Some thumb-rules in Contract Management:

a. General conditions of contract in many PUs and Government Departments require the commencement of a work within 7 days of receipt of the letter of acceptance of tender, and completion in stages, as per time-schedule of completion (to be agreed to with E-in-C etc. within one month of acceptance of tender).

This should be strictly enforced, and any default is to be recorded and communicated in writing to the contractor, promptly, and with the notice that the contractor will be held liable for the consequences of such default.

b. All extensions of time granted to the contractor should be against specific requests, in wring, and should be qualified so as not to prejudice your rights to recover liquidated damages for the delay and or to cancel the contract and make alternate arrangements, at the cost and the risk of the contractor. Similarly, such extensions granted should be without any additional financial implications to you.

c. All damages, monitory or otherwise, actually resulting from delays in performance/non-performance should be quantified and recorded promptly.

These should also be communicated to the contractor, simultaneously. Documents/evidence in support should be carefully preserved for possible legal scrutiny, at a later date and when the need arises.

d. All contract variations should be only by mutual consent and, recorded either as minutes signed by both parties or by exchange of letter. Minutes signed by both sides are excellent pieces of evidence to support any claims from your side. In all other modes of communication, such as telephone discussions, there should be a confirmatory file note etc. available, as evidence. It may also be advantageous to send to the contractor written confirmation of such communication.

e. As per general conditions of contract, in many organisations, all notices to the contractors are to be served either personally, at site, or by registered mail.

This should be strictly followed, in order to be legally effective. Wherever possible, acknowledgement should be obtained.

f. Sometimes, the GCC entitles you, under certain circumstances, to determine / terminate a contract. In all such cases, it would be preferable to do this by mutual consent, minutes signed by both parties.

If it must be done unilaterally by you, it is better that your lawyer is consulted before taking any action, more so when such cancellation is done while the contractual delivery time is not yet over.

g. Whenever a contract is cancelled / terminated and alternate agreement for supply or performance is to be made, it would be preferable to check on the legal aspects of such action, in order to ensure its legal validity.

h. All letters from contractors - which call for actions or sanctions or supply / delivery on your part - must be responded to, promptly.

In cases of difficulties / differences, these should be resolved by mutual agreement and confirmed in writing. This will avoid the contractor taking undue advantage of any unintended or innocent neglect to so respond.

i. Any unauthorized variation from contractual performance / obligations is to be recorded and intimated to the contractor, promptly, and followed up, effectively, and progress payments certified only after satisfactory compliance or explanations.

j. Whatever obligations you have undertaken to perform under a contract must be performed by you promptly and recorded.

Any delay in such events entitles the contractor to a corresponding delay in performing his obligations, besides likely cost escalation claims. Examples are, approval of drawing / samples, inspection, import licences, supply of your own materials or facilities, delivery of site, etc.

k. Any discrepancies by the contractor in following your instructions, any alteration in specifications and designs and extra work should be fully documented and got acknowledged by the contractor.

1. Wherever the contract requires that the contractor should submit regular progress report on the work to be done, any lapse should be immediately recorded and intimated to the contractor as breach of the contractual terms and with all the agreed consequences.

m. The contractor should be made fully aware of the inspection agency., inspection standards, inspection methods etc. at the time of executing the contract. Any failure to pass inspection or failure to offer goods / work promptly for inspection should be notified to the contractor, promptly, pointing out that it is a breach of the contract with all agreed consequences.

n. No casual or unauthorised promises or commitments should be made to the contractor at any stage since these can cause significant legal embarrassment to those who do it, when they are cited by the contractor as witnesses in any legal action.

In conclusion, it may be noted that all legal processes are observed more by "proof" and evidence" than by "truth". Therefore, it should be ensured that there is documentary evidence built-up as the execution of the contract progresses, and oral understandings and commitments are to be totally avoided.

BREACH OF CONTRACT AND REMEDIES

1. The breach of a contract arises from the failure or refusal to perform it. When there is a failure to perform an entire obligation, it is termed as a total breach of contract. When an agreement is broken only in part, it is termed as partial breach. If a party announces before his performance is due, his definite unwillingness or inability to fulfil the contractual obligation, it is termed "anticipatory breach". Any breach of contract without sufficient excuse or justification becomes actionable ie. a suit or other appropriate legal proceeding can be initiated for getting relief. The law of contract does not (at least in theory) seek to punish; its purpose is compensation and compensation alone.

2. Remedies available in law for the breach of contract are damages, specific performance and injunction, cancellation and rectification. Sections 73 and 74 of the Contract Act deal with damages.

When a party suffers loss or damage in consequence of a breach of contract, by non-performance or defective performance, he is entitled to recover compensation from the party breaking the contract. The principle is that the injured party should, as far as possible, be placed in the same position, in terms of money, as if the contract had been performed by the party, in default.

This is based on the doctrine of restitution, which is, that a person cannot unjustly enrich himself. The principle of restitution is not based on loss suffered by the plaintiff but on the benefit received by the defendant which he is wholly unjustified in retaining.

3. On default by a contracting party, a right to sue alone would arise. That right to sue will furnish a cause of action for the suit for damages. Therefore, a party who commits a breach of contract does not automatically incur any pecuniary liability. It would also not be true to say that the other party to the contract who complains of the breach has any amount due to him from the other party.

The only right which he has is the right to go to a court of law and recover damages. Also, no pecuniary liability arises till the court has determined that the party complaining of the breach is entitled to damages.

4. There is a difference in law between 'damage' and "damages". "Damages" is not the plural form of " "damage". Damage" means and includes loss of money, comfort, health or the like.

"Damages" means money compensation, claimed by the injured party, for the injuries suffered.

Damages may be termed as liquidated or unliquidated. 'Unliquidated damages' are compensatory in character.

This is ascertained with the fundamental consideration to place the innocent party in the position he would have occupied, had the contract been performed according to its terms.

'Liquidated damages' is the actual sum named in the contract, which the parties have themselves calculated would be a fair compensation, for breach of the contract.

It is clear that the purpose of liquidated damages is to compensate the injured party for the loss suffered.

The injured party has no right to make a profit out of this. It, therefore, follows that although parties may have agreed to a fixed sum payable as damages, if such sum exceeds the actual loss, the injured party will get nothing more than the actual loss suffered. Hence it is clear that, in India, there is no distinction between the two ways of naming a sum of compensation, as 'penalty' or as "liquidated damages".

5. Section 74 of the Indian Contract Act reads as follows:

"When a contract has been broken, if a sum is named in the contract as the amount to be paid in case of such breach, or if the contract contains any other stipulation by way of penalty, the party complaining of the breach is entitled, whether or not actual damage or loss is proved to have been caused thereby, to receive from the party who has broken the contract <u>reasonable compensation</u> not

exceeding the amount so named or as the case may be,
the penalty stipulated for". (Emphasis added)

6. The language of the section has made its interpretation difficult. The trouble is that, even now, the courts have not arrived at any clear or certain interpretation to make it absolutely free from difficulty. The section provides that reasonable compensation only is payable. At the same time, it also provides that the reasonable compensation is payable whether actual damage or loss is proved to have been caused by the breach. If it is a case of reasonable compensation, then surely such reasonableness would depend on the facts and circumstances of each case.

But the Section says that it makes no difference whether or not actual damage or loss is proved. It further says that the reasonable compensation is not to exceed the amount named in the contract. The words of the section give a wide discretion to the court in the assessment of damages.

Although the discretion of the court in the matter of reducing the amount of damages agreed upon is left unqualified, the expression "reasonable compensation" used in the Section necessarily implies that the discretion must be exercised with care, caution and on sound principles.

E.g.: the measure of damages for failure to complete a building in time, where time is the essence of the contract, is the rental value of the building for the period of delay and not the rent paid by the owner, during the delayed period, for the house he occupied. In some contracts, it may be possible for the court to assess the compensation but, in some others this assessment may be extremely difficult.

7. In cases where the reciprocal obligations of the opposite party are unfulfilled, there will not be any right for them to levy or claim damages, even if liquidated. It has been further held that, any stipulation for unliquidated damages in a contract gives rise only to a right to sue on default and no right to any amount.

8. It is the essence of 'liquidated damages' that it should run from a fixed date. It is, therefore, essential to specify time limit within which the performance is to be completed. It is not necessary to state that 'time shall be the essence of the contract'.

9. The owner may lose his right for liquidated damages in the following circumstances:

a. Provision for extension of time is made in the contract, but extension is not granted inspite of just reasons.

b. When any act of the owner itself renders it impossible for contractor to complete the work, on schedule.

c. If the Architect or the Engineer of the owner gives certificate of satisfactory completion and certifies the balance due to the Contractor.

Normally, right to liquidated damages excludes the right to claim unliquidated damages.

10. Construction contracts, usually, contain stipulation for forfeiture of earnest money or security deposit of the contractor if he commits breach of contract.

Usually earnest money paid along with the tender is forfeited if the contractor fails to keep the offer open for the period mentioned in the tender notice or fails to sign and complete the contract documents and furnish the security deposits specified in the tender notice.

11. 'Earnest Money' is the term commonly used in a contract where it is considered as an earnest to the bargain and creates by fear of its forfeiture a motive in the contractor to perform the rest of the contract. In short, it is a guarantee for the performance of the contract.

It is supposed to show an earnestness or ardent desire on the part of the contractor to go forward with the contract. In that sense, it is a security deposit for performance of the contract and, invariably, the terms of the contract do stipulate, that it will be converted into security deposit on signing of the contract by the contractor.

12. The right reserved in the terms of an invitation to tender to forfeit the earnest money for failure of the contractor to keep the offer open is clearly without consideration and not enforceable. The forfeiture of earnest money can be considered only after the tender is accepted and the contractor refuses to sign the agreement or perform it, because in that case, the acceptance of a tender converts it into a legally binding agreement and the contractor becomes liable for breach of it. Even in such cases the owner may not be entitled to forfeit automatically the earnest money. The situation gets even more complicated when the tender invitation reserves for the owner the right to reject any / all tenders or not to accept the lowest tender.

13. In most construction contracts, the practice of accepting bank guarantee in place of cash security is followed.

This has the advantage of the working capital of the contractor not getting locked up and, as a result thereof, the owner getting the benefit of a lower rate than the rates which the contractor would have quoted if he were to provide cash security.

But, when a demand is made for the encashment of a bank guarantee, the court is approached by the contractor to get an injunction to restrain the bank from making the payment to the owner.

A bank guarantee is very much like an irrevocable letter of credit and, the Courts will do the utmost to enforce it, except when it is obtained by fraud, coercion etc. The liability of the Bank under the guarantee is absolute.

14. Provision is also usually made in contracts to enable the owners to recover amounts due to them

from any other sums of the Contractor, in the hands of the owner. Such a clause has been held to be valid and binding on the parties.

15. Apart from damages, another relief which could be obtained through the Courts is injunction.

An injunction is an order made by the Court forbidding or restraining a person from doing a certain act or acts.

In general, an injunction forbids a person from doing certain acts, but, sometimes, it forbids the continuance of a wrongful state of affairs, that already exists. An injunction forbidding the continuance of an existing thing is called a mandatory injunction. An injunction can also be directory, in the sense that a person can be ordered to do certain positive acts. In short, an injunction is an order of court framed according to the circumstances and needs of the case, commanding an act which the Court regards as essential to justice or restraining an act which it considers as contrary to equity and good conscience.

16. Injunctions can be temporary (also called interlocutory) or perpetual. Interlocutory injunctions continue until the hearing of the case, upon merits, generally, "until further orders". Perpetual injunctions

form part of the decree made after the hearing on merits.
The Perpetual injunction, in effect, concludes a right. The
interlocutory injunction is merely to preserve the 'status
quo ante' until the hearing of the case. The law relating
to injunction in India is incorporated in the Specific
Relief Act and the Code of Civil Procedure. Whereas,
perpetual injunctions come within the purview of the
Specific Relief Act, temporary injunctions are issued
under the provisions of the Code of Civil Procedure. The
question of injunction in building contracts, generally,
arises when an employer wants to exercise his right of
forfeiture contained in the contract against his contractor
on account of default committed by the latter in the
performance of his contract. It is difficult for Court to
look after the acts and conduct of a builder, nor can the
courts say how far he departs from properly executing the
work. Where the case is one in which the personal skill is
an important factor, the courts will not be able to enforce
it.

Besides, if a contractor is unlawfully dismissed, he has the remedy of getting compensation by way of damages, and in such cases specific performance will not be granted by the Court.

Thus, no injunction can issue against an employer in a building contract at the instance of the contractor.

17. In these building and engineering contracts, it is also usual to insert provisions empowering the employer to forfeit certain rights or property of the contractor on the occurrence of certain events.

For example, the employer may reserve the right to take possession of the work till then performed and to complete the work either by himself or by employing others. Provision may also be incorporated to take possession of or retain the property of the contractor, such as material, plant or money already due to him. In the absence of express terms, the contractor has merely a license to enter upon the site of the employer to execute the works.

Such a license can be revoked by the employer at any time. But such revocation, if not justified under the terms of the contract, will render the owner liable for damages. In cases where the contractor commits a fundamental breach, this right can be exercised by the employer. Under the general law, the contractor also has a power identical to that of the employer to treat the contract as repudiated, where the employer has shown an intention to abandon it.

18. The usual contingencies where the power of forfeiture may be exercised by the employer can be listed as follows: -

1. Contractor not commencing the work.

2. Not regularly proceeding with the work for a certain fixed period.

3. Not proceeding to the satisfaction of the employer.

4. Not proceeding for any reason independently of prevention by the employer.

5. Not exercising due diligence and dispatch as will enable the work to be completed in time.

6. Not completing as stipulated.

7. Not complying with the orders and directions given by the architect or engineer.

8. Not complying with the specifications, stipulations, conditions, or drawings.

9. Being guilty of default in fulfilling the contract.

10. Leaving the work unfinished.

11. Failing after due notice, to rectify defective works.

12. Removing material from the site, unauthorizedly.

19. Apart from these instances, there can be various other cases in which the right to forfeiture of the contract may arise. Where a contract contains a clause conferring an express power of termination upon the contractor, the conditions upon which the exercise of that power is generally made is dependent on the failure of the

employer to make interim payments within the specified period, bankruptcy of the employer, non- release of work-fronts or materials, in time, etc.

20. It is a matter of each case, depending upon the terms of the contract, that will justify the determination of the contract. Under the general law, some acts or omissions of any one of the parties to contract may justify the other in regarding the contract as repudiated.

21. The power to forfeit or terminate the contract must be exercised in an unqualified manner.

Where under the terms of the contract, the ascertainment of the event sufficient to terminate the contract is left to the employer himself, the rule is that he must act reasonably.

22. The question of reasonableness, to a great extent, depends on the particular circumstances of the case. The clause in the contract will be very strictly construed by courts.

Sometimes the contract may provide the right or duty of deciding whether the event has happened, giving right to forfeiture to a third person such as the engineer or the architect.

23. The power to forfeit for delay often arises upon the occurrence of either or both of two events. viz., delay in progress and failure to complete the work in time. Forfeiture is a term commonly and somewhat loosely used. Generally, it means the taking possession of works, completely ousting the Contractor from the site. If the employer purports to terminate the contract, or to take possession of the property of the contractor, when the contract does not empower him to do so or, if he exceeds his power or, if the stipulated notice is not given, the Contractor has an option to sue the owner for damages.

ARBITRATION

The subject matter for today is the "Need, importance and relevance of arbitration". The art and science of arbitration is a living and changing thing. The essence of arbitration is the settlement of disputes by a tribunal chosen by the parties themselves, rather than by the Courts constituted by the State. The popularity of arbitration as a mode of settling disputes is due to the fact that "the arbitration is regarded as speedier, more informal and cheaper than conventional judicial procedure and provides a forum more convenient to the parties who can choose the time and place for conducting arbitration and the procedure. Further, where the dispute concerns a technical matter, the parties can select an arbitrator who possesses appropriate special qualifications or skills in the trade".

As a concept and as a process, arbitration is well embedded in commercial practices and social life.

Arbitration is the means by which parties to a dispute get the same settled through the intervention of a third person, but without having recourse to a court of law. When two persons agree to have a dispute settled through arbitration, what they really mean is that the actual resolution of the dispute will rest with a third person called the arbitrator.

The essence of arbitration, therefore, is that it is the arbitrator who decides the case and not the ordinary civil courts established by the state. The law of arbitration, is based upon the principle of referring the disputes to a domestic tribunal substituted in the place of a regular Court.

Thus, arbitration can be defined as a reference to the decision of one or more persons called arbitrators of a particular matter in difference or dispute between the parties. It can be defined as the determination of a matter in dispute by the award of one or more persons called arbitrators.

Halsbury defines "arbitration" as the reference of dispute or difference between not less than than two parties for determination after hearing both sides in a judicial manner by a person or persons other than a Court. An equivalent in the old Indian system for arbitration is Panchayat. In India arbitration has a very ancient heritage. Indian civilisation expressly encouraged the settlement of differences by Tribunals chosen by the parties themselves. In the Western world also arbitration has a very long history. The Greeks attached particular importance to arbitration.

Submission of disputes to the decision of private persons was recognised also under the Roman law known by the name of compromysm (compromise), arbitration was a mode of settling controversies much favoured in the civil law of the continent.

The attitude of English law towards arbitration has been fluctuating from stiff opposition to moderate welcome. The common law courts looked jealously at agreements to submit disputes to extra-judicial determination.

It was the exigencies of business that brought about an increasing demand for commercial arbitration in England. The realities of business in due course brought about a change in judicial attitude. In India the history of statute relating to arbitration begins with the regulations under the East India Company made for the Presidency of Bengal, Madras and Bombay.

These regulations were later expanded in the Civil Procedure Act of 1859. In 1940, an Arbitration Act was passed for the whole of British India. On 26.01.1950 the Act was extended to the whole of India except the Part B States.

That Act was repealed by the Arbitration and Conciliation Ordinance 1996 (Act 8 of 1996) which came into force on 25.01.1996 and on its expiry Arbitration and Conciliation Ordinance (Act 11) of 1996 and thereafter during the Parliament session in 1996 came to be enacted as the Arbitration and Conciliation Act, 1996.

What is meant by arbitration is not defined in the Arbitration Act, but an arbitration agreement is defined as an agreement by the parties to submit to arbitration all or certain disputes which have arisen or which may arise between the parties. Ronald Bernstein defines an arbitration as under

"Where two or more persons agree that a dispute or a potential dispute between them shall be decided in a legally binding way by one or more impartial persons in a judicial manner, that is, upon evidence put before him or them, the agreement is called an arbitration agreement or a submission to arbitration". Sec.7(5) of the Act expressly provides that reference to a document containing an arbitration clause would constitute an arbitration agreement.

When after a dispute has arisen, it is put before such person for decision the procedure is called an arbitration and decision when made is called an award. Sometimes the submission instead of being voluntary is imposed by statute. Such arbitrations are called statutory arbitrations.

There are more than 25 central Acts providing for statutory arbitration in India. For example, under the Co-operative Societies Act and under the Telegraph Act etc. arbitration is provided for statutorily. The provisions of these statutes to the extent inconsistent with the provisions of the Arbitration Act will prevail over the provisions of the Arbitration Act.

Arbitration offers definite advantages that litigation from its very nature can never provide. Courts have always adopted a conservative approach to problems. The Courts of law are put into a strait jacket as it must follow fixed procedure and fixed rules of evidence. Arbitration, on the other hand, is more informal. The Evidence Act is not applicable to arbitration. The Civil Procedure Code has no application. The arbitrator need only proceed in a manner conforming to justice, equity and good conscience. He is not henched in by any formulated rules.

One of the major advantages of arbitration is that an expert arbitral tribunal can be selected considering the field of dispute, so much so, the entire procedure can be conducted without the intervention of expert lawyers, with major gains in speed and economy. Thus, many disputes as to quality in commodity trades, many disputes arising out of construction contract etc. can be settled through arbitration in a speedy manner at lesser cost and more quickly than through courts.

Arbitrators and judges are similar in the business of dispensing justice - the judge in the public sector and the arbitrator in the private sector. The public legal system of any country represents a compromise between conflicting demands for quality, speed, and cheapness of the decision - making process.

Of these, quality of decision making is usually given the highest priority. Speed of the decision and cheapness have suffered considerably.

Litigants had to que up for the services of the Court and to accept the delay, the inconvenience and often the loss consequent on the delay.

However, it must be said that the result of any arbitration depends upon the personality of the arbitrator. The arbitrator should always bear in mind the range of procedures open to him so as to be able to suggest to the parties the course which will save costs without reducing to an unacceptable extent the quality of the decision-making process. To summaries, properly conducted arbitrations give acceptable results with speed and thoroughness at relatively lesser costs. As there is no right of appeal in Courts, the decision gains finality saving further time and costs.

However, in practice, one sometimes comes across disputes where the issue is how much is to be awarded or the assessment of damages for breach of contract.

Here the proceedings generally tend to be bedeviled by wild overestimates for the claimant or underestimate for the respondents. The amount of claim is magnified and costs over-stated.

Proceedings which should be an amicable attempt to resolve a genuine difference of opinion are turned into an adversarial and cynical game in which it is thought that victory will go to the most convincing liar or at least a long drawn out battle in which the initial wild exaggerations have first to be demolished before the real dispute is explored.

What is termed in legal parlance as the 'forest technique of pleading is used by claimants. The farrago of obscurities in the contract is highlighted - all instructions and drawings are without exception alleged to have caused disturbance and additional loss or to have been issued late in an attempt to avoid the exposure to the critical examination involved in a more selective analysis of the claim.

Such disputes are fertile soil for the lawyers. If the rival claims are small and each side believes that the difference results from a genuine difference of opinion the parties may be normally content to appear in person or by an employee before the arbitrator. They may even square up the disputes behind the back of the arbitrator. The resulting procedure shows arbitration at its most useful. But if the difference is great and one or both the parties think that the other is knowingly exaggerating, the tendency is to appoint advocate partly because the amount in issue is such as to justify the additional expense involved or partly because of the fear that unless every possible point in defense is taken the exaggeration of the opponent may be accepted by the arbitrator also partly because the task of exposing by cross examination the exaggerations of the claimant and his witnesses is the expert task of a lawyer.

The relevance of arbitration, its importance and its needs can never be over-emphasized.

The rapid and phenomenal growth of commerce and
industry and the complex and varied problems thrown
out by them can find solution only through arbitration.
Conventional courts are ill equipped to meet the needs.

ENFORCEMENT OF ARBITRAL AWARDS

An arbitration comes into being as a result of an enforceable agreement. An agreement enforceable under law is called a contract. To be enforceable the agreement must be made by free consent of the parties. Parties are said to consent when they agree upon the same thing in the same sense. A consent can be said to be free when it is not induced by coercion, undue influence, fraud, misrepresentation or mistake as to matter of fact essential to the agreement. The onus of proving that free consent was not given is upon the party asserting it. An arbitration agreement is void if a party is a minor or is not of sound mind or is disqualified from contracting by any law to which he is subject. When both the parties to the agreement are under a mutual mistake as to a matter of fact essential to the agreement, the agreement is void. An arbitration agreement of which the object or consideration is unlawful is void.

The consideration or object is unlawful if it is forbidden by law or is of such a nature that if permitted it would defeat the provisions of any law or is fraudulent or involves or implies injury to the person or property of another or the courts regard it as immoral or opposed to public policy.

The Arbitration Act provides that an arbitration agreement should be in writing. Hence, no oral arbitration is possible in India.

It is not necessary to constitute the agreement in any single document.

It can spread over so many documents. A contract may by express language incorporate the provisions of another contract containing an arbitration clause. If so, the arbitration clause will be deemed to have been incorporated in the contract.

If a contract is illegal and void an arbitration clause which is one of its terms is also rendered illegal.

The taint of illegality attaches to every part of the contract. Thus an arbitration clause for stifling prosecution or involving criminal proceedings is of no effect.

It was mentioned earlier that an arbitration agreement is an agreement to submit present and/or future disputes to arbitration. The existence of a dispute is one of the essential elements for invoking an arbitration. A dispute implies assertion of a right by one party and the refutation thereof by another.

The refutation may be express or implied and may be by words or conduct. Failure to pay under a claim or right is a dispute. Failure to perform the contract in time may lead to an inference of refutation and denial of the right by the other party. Such conduct and such silence may be more eloquent than words and will show that the party is disputing liability.

There can be no dispute unless there is a denial of a claim. There is a dispute whenever there is a matter capable of being agitated in a civil court. It is not exactly necessary that the claim should be valid or sustainable in a court of law.

The decision of an arbitrator is called an award. Our law does not impose any legal requirement as to the form of a valid award. The only requirement is that it should be in writing, signed by the arbitrator.

But, if the agreement contains requirements as to the form of the award then those requirements should be met. For example, if the agreement says that the arbitrator need not give a speaking award, the award need not contain reasons to support his conclusions. Otherwise in all cases an arbitrator is obliged to give a speaking award.

As a matter of fact, there are certain basic requirements for an award. The award should identify the parties by name.

The date of the award should be shown at some place of the award. If there are more than one arbitrator all should sign the award. But if there is omission of any signature the reasons should be stated. There is no requirement of witnesses attesting the award. The award should be certain, i.e., one should be able to clearly understand the arbitrator's decision by reading the award.

The Arbitration Act defines an award as including an interim award. This is a formal definition.

In essence an award is the judgement of the arbitrator on the merits of the case.

The Arbitration Act confers on the arbitrators the right to conduct the proceedings in the manner they consider appropriate. It has been held that parties by consent can also agree on the procedure to be followed by the arbitral tribunal in conducting the proceedings.

Arbitrators are not at liberty to make an award without giving reasons unless it is so stipulated in the agreement.

The powers of the Court to interfere with the awards are now very limited. Section 34 of the Arbitration Act provides for an application to the Court for setting aside an award under the following circumstances: -

a) Incapacity of party

b) Invalidity of the agreement

c) Want of proper notice

d) Award deals with disputes not referred to arbitration

e) Arbitral Tribunal was defective in composition

f) Subject matter not capable of arbitration

g) Award conflicts with public policy.

An award can be enforced as such because it is now equated with a decree of the Court. A party who wishes to enforce the award can file it before the Court and it will be treated as a decree unless set aside in an application under section 34.

An application for setting aside shall not be made after three months of the receipt of the award or after three months of an application under section 33 to the arbitration for any correction of the award. An arbitrator has got the power to file the award and the connected papers in Court 'suo-motu' at any time. There is no period of limitation fixed for it.

The arbitrator has to give a signed copy of the award to the parties. After receiving the award the concerned party has to apply to the Court to execute the award and obtain reliefs. The court will issue notice to the judgement debtor. After receipt of notice if the judgement debtor does not appear before Court, ex-parte execution may be ordered granting the relief prayed for in the Petition.

If the judgement debtor appears and files objection, the objection will be heard and disposed of and only thereafter necessary relief will be granted by the Court. Under Order XXI of the Code of Civil Procedure a judgement debtor can be proceeded against either in person or against his property.

Personal execution is by arresting the judgement debtor.
A judgement debtor can be imprisoned for a period of
three months. The expenses for this have to be met by the
decree holder. Execution against property is by attaching
and selling through Court the saleable interest of the
judgement debtor in the property. If a judgement debtor
has no assets, he is safe in spite of a decree against him
as he cannot even be imprisoned for the decree debt.

The procedure for enforcing foreign awards is as per Part
II of the present Act and incorporates the Geneva
Convention of 1927 and the New York Convention of
1958. Pursuant to this any person interested in enforcing
a foreign award shall apply to a Court having jurisdiction
over the subject matter of the award.

The parties seeking to enforce a foreign award must
produce:

a) The original award or a duly authenticated copy
   thereof.

b) Evidence proving that the award has become final and

c) Such evidence as is necessary to prove that the award is a foreign award.

Even though arbitration is a more efficacious, equitable and quick remedy, it is often misused to make unlawful gains. One of our judges remarked:

"The malady of the racket of arbitration is rampant in our country. Arbitration of late is being considered as a sure way to overnight riches and affluence. It has become a big business.

A judge can no longer be impervious to the winds that blow outside leaving the seclusion of his ivory tower, he should come to the streets to feel the total push and pressure of the cosmos.

In a social welfare state the need is social justice. It is true that today in every department the social value of the rule of law becomes a test of growing power and importance."

Instances of arbitrators awarding huge amounts by way of non-speaking awards was prevalent in many departments, such as PWD, Irrigation and Electricity Boards and the Kerala Government was forced to take away the Arbitration clause forcing the contractors to seek remedy through court. If a suit is to be filed, Court fee has to be paid and the case has to be established through incontrovertible evidence. If one court goes wrong there is an appellate court. Details and reasons are to be given by the Court for its findings. Because of these only genuine claims will be brought by the parties in a court of law. Avaricious contractors and dishonest arbitrators have given a bad name for the process of arbitration. Hence an honest man dreads arbitration even more than the dreaded lawsuits.

The general rule in matters of arbitration awards is that where parties have agreed upon an arbitration thereby displacing a Court of law, they must accept the award for good or worse.

In such cases, the discretion of the Court will not be readily exercised and will be strictly confined to the specific grounds set out under section 34.

The arbitrator is the final judge on fact. Adequacy of evidence is not to be examined. The arbitrator is not bound by technical rules of evidence. The Court cannot investigate the reasonableness of the arbitrator's reasons. In deciding a controversy, the arbitrator works in an environment which is different from that of the judge. The ropes and pulleys that he uses in the arbitral process are different from the foot-rules and set-squares that the judge uses in the judicial process.

ON CONTRACT LABOUR

Chapter IV of the Constitution of India contains the Directive Principles of State Policy. These principles though not enforceable, judicially, like the fundamental rights are treated as fundamental in the governance of the country. The State has a duty to apply these principles in making laws.

The Contract Labour (Regulation and Abolition) Act, 1970 was passed as a measure to achieve some of the objectives contained in the directive principles. Human beings are exploited by unscrupulous persons practicing the labour contract system by which the benefits of the sweat and work of a contract labour are taken away by the contractor and the employer. The preamble to the Act states the purpose of the Act viz.(i) to regulate contract labour where necessary and (ii) to abolish contract labour in certain circumstances. For this purpose, the Act requires the registration of the principal employer and the licensing of the contractor and the employment of contract labour through licensed contractors. If the employment of contract labour is done through any other intermediary, they would be deemed to have been employed by the principal employer himself. However, the Act nowhere provides that such labour employed through a contractor would become employees of the principal employer himself.

It legalizes the employment of contract labour by any establishment through a contractor provided the establishment obtains the requisite registration as principal employer and provided also that the intermediary contractor obtains a license.

In the absence of such a registration or license, the workman would ipso facto' attain the status of the workman of the establishment itself, but the Act nowhere specifically provides that such employees employed through a contractor would become employees of the principal employer.

Temporary labour is employable in industry for work of a purely temporary nature or as a temporary substitute of a permanent worker who is absent. Contract labour is usable only in activities which do not form the normal part of an industry's main functions. Both these provisions of law are based on the need to prevent adventurous employers who tend to resort to these types of employment to deny permanency and other fringe benefits of permanency to temporary and contract labour. Normally, resort to such labour is done in the areas of housekeeping and sanitation, pollution control, security services, canteen etc. and the contractor gets these assignments done on an ongoing basis, but supervised by the management.

Similar is the case when time-bound, penalty-oriented jobs are being done by an employer or when there is unstructured absenteeism deliberately resorted to by permanent workers.

In all these cases, it is seen that the quantum of work done by contract labour is invariably more than that done by similarly employed permanent workmen.

If use of contract labour is banned and strictly enforced, almost 80% of the industries, especially public sector industries, will have to close down. This is not because managements are nasty or unfair, but the Act does not reckon with industrial compulsions.

Our laws relating to labour are based on social justice, not industrial justice and equity. Because of this, they cannot be enforced and are rarely enforced. The fact of the matter is that, in the context of to-day's high industrial wage costs, contract labour to some extent is unavoidable and is a reality to be reckoned with. All that an industry should attempt to do is to conform to the laws as much as possible, in order to avoid embarrassing and expensive penal action by the enforcing authority.

We shall now see the salient provisions of the Act, and I will only try to present them as statutory obligations and guidelines to be followed by you as Principal Employer:

REGISTRATION

If you are a Principal Employer of an establishment engaging 20 or more contract labour, get your establishment registered under the Act for which apply in the prescribed form to the Registering Officer, pay the fees prescribed depending on the number of contract labour and furnish any additional information required by the Registration Officer. Intimate any change that may occur and get the Registration Certificate amended accordingly

LICENCE

a) Get your contractor(s) obtain a license from the Licensing Officer

b) Give the requisite certificate in form V to your contractor for obtaining license.

c) Ensure that he obtains license and renews it every year as required.

ENSURE THAT THE CONTRACTOR:

a) Pays minimum wages fixed by the government if, any, or

b) Pays wages as may be fixed by the Commissioner of Labour.

c) In their absence pays fair wages to contract labour.

d) Complies with all the legal requirements of the Act.

c) Maintains various registers and records, displays notices, abstracts of the Acts, Rules etc. f Issues employment card to his workmen, etc.

SUPERVISE:

Appoint a Representative to supervise the payment of wages by the Contractors) to the Contract Labour.

In case of failure to pay wages by the Contractor to his men, the Principal employer shall arrange to pay the legal dues of the contract labour and recover the money from the sum payable to the contractor

FACILITIES

Ensure that Contractor provides the following services and facilities:

1. Canteen (if employing 100 or more workmen in one place) and if the work is likely to last for 6 months or more.

2. Rest rooms where the workmen are required to halt at night and the work is likely to last for 3 months or more.

3. Requisite number of latrines and urinals - separate for men and women.

4. Drinking water.

5. Washing facilities.

6. First Aid box

FURTHER

a) If the principal employer can allow the contract labour to use above mentioned facilities which he has provided to his direct men, it is not necessary for the contractor to provide them separately to the contract labour

b) If the contractor fails to provide the above facilities, the Principal Employer has to provide these facilities to the contract labour and recover costs for the same from the contractor.

From the industrial relations point of view it is desirable to extend the same facilities to contract labour which the principal employer is providing to his direct men like canteen, rest room, latrines/urinals, drinking water, washing and first aid facilities and you may make adjustment in the rates/money payable to the contractor for providing these services directly to the contract labour.

REGISTER

Maintain register of contractors in Form VII and produce the same when required by the Inspector.

AVOID DEFAULT

In short, ensure that the contractors) comply with all the formalities and requirements of law and there is no default on his part.

LIABILITY

If you fail to register your establishment or the contractor does not obtain a licence, the contract labour shall be deemed to be your direct workmen and you will be fully liable for the wages, services and facilities of the contract labour etc. You are really buying trouble for the Company and for yourself.

INTIMATION

As soon as the work of the contractor with you is over, ask him to send an intimation to the Inspector regarding the completion of his job. For caution, you may also send the intimation, in addition

PRECAUTIONS

While entrusting work on contract basis to a contractor, explicitly stipulate that he and his subcontractors shall fully comply with the following enactments: -

a) Contract Labour Regulation and Abolition Act, 1970

b) Minimum Wages Act, if applicable

c) Payment of Wages Act, if applicable

d) ESI Act, 1948, if applicable

e) EPF Act, 1952, if applicable

f) Any other law, if applicable

2. The contract should specify that the Contractor shall be solely and fully responsible for all the contract labour employed by him or by his sub-contractors.

3. In case of any failure to comply with a statutory liability by the Contractor, the same shall be done by the Principal Employer and the expenses so incurred by the Principal employer shall be deducted from the sums payable to the contractor and if no money is due, the same shall be recoverable from the contractor otherwise.

4. To avoid any industrial relations problems that may arise out of employment of contract labour vis-a-vis the direct workmen of the Principal Employer or their Union(s), it is better to come to a clear understanding (by a written agreement wherever felt necessary and possible) with direct workmen and/or their Union(s) regarding areas/function/processes which will be carried on with the help of contract labour and stipulate that they shall not dabble with areas of contract labour.

5. In case of any confrontation with the direct workmen on any issue, the first attack will be on contract labour employment and the Principal employer should be ready with a contingency plan to deal with the situation.

6. Wherever the contract labour organizes and raises any demand for not only improvement of their service/conditions but also their absorption by the Principal Employer, advise the Contractor to improve the service/working conditions of his contract labour and enhance the contract rates to enable the contractor to bear the additional burden to the extent possible.

7. In case your own Union raises a demand for abolition of contract labour and employment of direct workmen, resist it to the last, lobby with the authorities concerned, Advisory Board, particularly the representatives of the employers on the Board with a view to persuading them not to recommend abolition of contract labour in the concerned process/work etc. which are carried on, on a regular basis.

8. With a view to avoid the contingency mentioned in clause 7 above, ensure that the Contractor not only complies with all the labour laws applicable to him both in letter and spirit, but also offers slightly better terms

and conditions to his labour and keeps a constant watch

on and touch with his

9. Wherever the contract labour is not covered by SI,

advise the contractor to fully insure them under

Workmen's Compensations Acts, cover himself against

all claims and extend the accidental insurance benefit to

the injured workmen.

10. Be careful in entrusting work on contract basis to

well established and reputed contractors and not to

novices even though it may mean paying slightly higher

rates to the contractors.

11. Finally, you keep your men, the contractor(s) and the

contract labour happy by being fair, considerate and yet

firm and that will pay the principal Employer rich

dividends in the long run.

§§§§§§§§§§